Helen Orme is a successful author of fiction and non-fiction, particularly for reluctant and struggling readers. She has written over fifty books for Ransom Publishing.

Helen was a teacher for nearly thirty years. She worked as a Special Educational Needs Co-ordinator in a large comprehensive school, as an advisory teacher for IT and as teacher-in-charge for a pupil referral unit. These experiences have been invaluable in her writing.

Street**Wise**

The Best Thing Ever

Helen Orme

Ransom

LEISURE AND CULTURE DUNDEE	
C00726129X	
Bertrams	02/07/2014
	£6.99
ARD	

Street**Wise**

The Best Thing Ever
by Helen Orme

Published by Ransom Publishing Ltd.
Radley House, 8 St. Cross Road, Winchester, Hampshire SO23 9HX, UK
www.ransom.co.uk

ISBN   978 184167 329 5
First published in 2014

CONTENTS

ONE

I Hate School

Liam grabbed his school bag and stormed out, slamming the door behind him.

He was fed up. It was always the same; *nag, nag, nag.* He couldn't do anything right.

He kicked an old Coke can into the
gutter. It bounced up and hit a parked
car.

'Oy! You!'

He turned quickly, then grinned. It was
Simon.

Simon caught him up and hit him
across the shoulders.

'What's happening then?' He looked at
Liam's face. 'What's up, mate?'

'It's them!' Liam jerked his head towards his house. 'They never let up.'

'What is it this time?'

'The usual – school. I hate school.'

They reached the main road.

'Got to go,' said Simon. 'See you.'

Liam made up his mind. 'Hey, wait for me,' he yelled. 'Where are you going?'

'Down town.'

'How about we go to the arcade, then?'

Liam really enjoyed the arcade games.

They were much better than any of the

computer games he'd got.

He stuffed his jacket into his rucksack.

'Quick,' he said. 'There's the bus.'

TWO

Go On, Try It

The time passed quickly at the arcade.

Liam had soon used up all his money.

'Here,' said Simon. He gave him a

tenner.

'I'll give it back tomorrow,' said Liam.

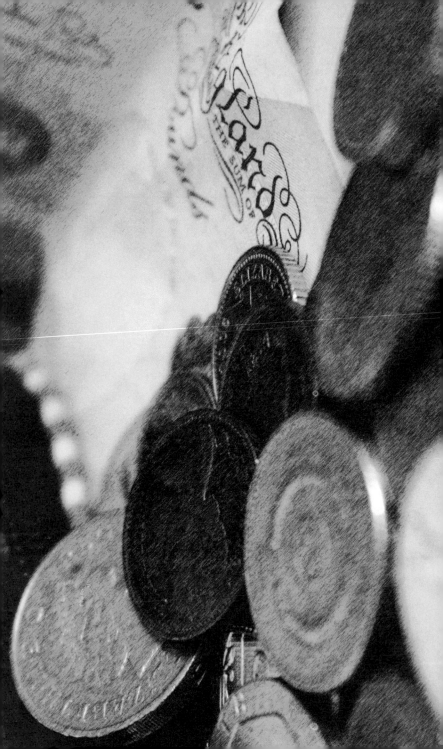

He knew Simon hadn't got a job.

'No worries,' said Simon. 'When you're ready.'

'How come you've got money to give away?' asked Liam. 'You've never had any spare before.'

'Easy,' Simon laughed. 'I get it here.'

'I didn't know you had a job.'

'I don't. I play the machines. You waste your money on games. You should try the pay-out ones.'

Simon led Liam over to the rows of slot machines. He pulled a handful of coins from his pocket. He gave a few to Liam.

'Go on, try it.'

Liam pushed the coin into the slot and hit the flashing button.

He stood grinning as money poured out of the machine. This was the best thing ever.

*****

When Liam got home, he was in

trouble. The school had phoned.

'Where were you?' shouted his mum.

'What were you doing?'

Liam glared at his mum. 'Nothing.'

The row went on. And on!

THREE

The Big One

At last Liam was free. No more exams.

No more school. He could do what he

liked. And what he liked was to go down

to the arcade and play the slot machines.

Sometimes he won and that was great,

but more often he didn't.

He hated being at home. They were still angry about him bunking off and wouldn't give him any more money.

'Get a job,' said his dad. As if it was that easy!

'I'll pay you to do some stuff around the house,' said his mum. 'You can clean out the garage and take the rubbish to the dump. Then you can do some gardening.

It'll keep you busy while I'm at work.'

Liam decided he would do anything if he could get some money, but mum was pretty mean with the pay. It just about kept him going in arcade visits.

Then it happened. The big one. He had never seen so many pound coins in one place.

Now he had enough to make a whole lot more. He wouldn't do any more jobs.

'You don't give me enough,' he said to his

mum and dad.

FOUR

They'd Never Notice

Liam needed more money.

He started hunting around the house.

He found a few pounds. Money that had

been left lying around. The odd pound

from his mum's purse.

cash ca

18 8644 01

RES 07/17

R
7529855 BRANCH 010

But it still wasn't enough. There was

no more. He'd searched everywhere.

He went into his parents' bedroom.

Nothing there, except his dad's bank

card.

He picked it up and looked at it.

Could he?

He knew his dad's PIN. He always used

the same one.

*****

At the cash machine Liam took out a hundred pounds. They'd never notice!

He put the card back carefully. The money would last for days.

But not many days. Liam didn't have another big win.

He looked for his dad's card again but it wasn't there.

He couldn't stand it. He had to have money.

Then he had an idea. Mum had a card too. It was the weekend, so she was home. He found her card. This time he'd take more – much more.

He got all he could. Not enough! He'd try some other hole-in-the-wall machines.

He went to a few more, but then something awful happened. The machine wouldn't give him any money. It wouldn't give him the card back, either.

What could he do? There was only one place to go. Back to the arcade. Maybe if he won enough he could pay them back and they wouldn't mind too much.

Everything would be all right. He knew it would.

Questions on the Story

◆ Why did Liam start going to the arcade?

◆ Why did Simon encourage him to try the machines that paid out money?

◆ Why did Liam think that he would
get away with 'borrowing' money
from his parents?

Discussion
Points

◆ We know that drugs and alcohol are addictive. Can things you *do*, such as computer games or slot machines, be addictive too?

◆ Were Liam's parents at fault in any way? What should they have done?

◆ Is Liam an addict?

Activities

◆ Imagine that Liam loses. He steals money from a total stranger and is caught.

Write what he says when he tries to explain himself to the police.

♦ Imagine Liam has another friend that tries to persuade him to stop.

Write out the conversation.

♦ Design a survey on gambling.

Include various forms of gambling, including online gambling (Internet websites and apps).

The survey should ask people for their views.